ARRIVAL PRESS

NORTH WEST CHORUS

1992

First published in Great Britain in 1992 by
ARRIVAL PRESS
3 Wulfric Square, Bretton,
Peterborough, PE3 8RF

Foreword

Arrival Press was formed in 1991 to promote the writing of poetry, often previously unpublished, from the thousands of contemporary, novice and established poets - old and young alike.

North West Chorus reflects the intriguing and entertaining variety of subjects poets are writing about today.

I'm sure you will enjoy reading this anthology as much as I have; and I hope it presents a fitting and lasting testimony to poets throughout the North West of the Country.

Contents

Fencing

Hold it in your hand,
Feel its warmth and weight,
See there how the grain
Is bent around a knot
Which proves it is real wood.
Please do not look so shocked -
I thought you understood.
From which world does it come?
From Earth of course - where else?
I don't see many trees
Out here on Mars, my friend.
Of course I know it's banned!
I had to risk my life
To bring it here to you;
You'll keep it in a safe
Under firm lock and key
And save it for the sight
Of those you really trust.
I wonder if you know
What humans of the past
Who carved it from the tree
Would use this fencepost for?
They'd chop it into bits
And throw it on the fire.

John Francis Haines

1

Fantasy Dream

I would very much like
to write a poem
or a very good sonnet
But no matter how
hard I try it seems
that I just cannot.

Like most other poets
and writers I dream,
of writing something great.
But deep down inside I know
I might not have got
what it really takes.

I will try to write a pop
song that is not so very
good and wont even rhyme.
That will make me into a
millionaire, in such
a very short time.

Then I'd live out in
Hawaii, or on the sands
of Bondi beach.
And carry on writing
modern pop songs, and
feel just like a thief.

With money troubles gone
I'll relax and good poetry
I should write.
Alas this was not to be because
that was a dream I had
when I went to bed last night.

John Joseph Cox

Little Angels!

I've been blessed with two young children
And it's very plain to see
They're not little angels,
They were never meant to be.

'Mum you get so cross with me
When I hang my clothes up...on the floor,
I wander all around the house
And never shut the door.'

'I haven't learnt my spellings Mum,
I've left my book behind.
I've got to learn my tables too,
We're up to number nines.'

'My duffle coats all muddy
And the pockets are all ripped.
I wasn't fighting, honest Mum,
I think I must have tripped.'

'I can't find my tie Mum
I've only got one shoe,
Have you seen my wellingtons?
I've lost my school bag too.'

'Mum I wake at six o'clock
But I can't stay in bed.
Why can't you wake up mum
And play with me instead?'

Yes those are my two children
They'd thwart any Mother's plan
Still I love those little rascals
Young Matthew and Johan.
Marilyn Ashcroft

The Lake

I wander through each country lane,
Near where the vast lake does flow,
And see in flower's, drops of rain,
Wet and shiny, wild they grow.

In every petal on every flower,
In every bee's pouch of pollen,
In every cloud, in every shower,
The voice of the wind has spoken.

How the lake breathes a sigh,
Every whispering song calls,
And the voice flows by,
Runs in ripples down sandy walls.

But beauty ages I fear,
How the youthful vandals curse,
Blasts the land with a tear,
And soiled with litter is nature's purse.

Denise Russell

Ode to Garnett

My name is Garnett Swindlehurst,
of champions I'm the very first,
on Shrewsbury Drive I live with my mum.
Whilst next door lives Ben, who is my chum.

We go for walkies in the fields
Where all the rounding up appeals,
Then Ben and I to the garden run,
Oh! we do have lots and lots of fun.

Until were called to stop the play
As we romp on borders gay,
We don't mean any harm at all!
Oh! there she is again - her call!

Monday is my training day
With another Ben, I've time to play,
I love my mum - my mum loves me,
Oh! why can't we always agree.

My Auntie Winnie gets me meat
I look for her across the street,
My two paws over the garden wall
Then on her, we usually call.

On Wednesdays when Margaret's up
She loves me too - a lucky pup!
We go across to have a chat,
But really it's to get her hat.

Margaret F Whiteside

5

The Beat

And so the poet danced on
For several years
Gliding in and out of circles

Walking, listening, learning
Testing the art of
Sociability from time to time

But always gliding
Above
Without
So seldom coming to land
Within

Fluttering
Flirting
Dancing for the music
And when the music stops

Just gliding on to pasture's new

- New rhythm
- New pace
- Perhaps new shoes

Shall one day
The poet write his own tune?
And set up home
To woo the passer's by
To come make music
        for a little while.

Gillian Ann Atherton

Come and Join the Boys Brigade

Come on lads don't be afraid
Come and join the Boy's Brigade,
Learn self respect and good behaviour
Come and worship Christ our saviour.

Come on lads, don't be afraid
Come and join our church parade,
Our anchor is steadfast and sure
Grounded deep to make hearts pure.

Come on lads, don't be afraid
Come and join the Boy's Brigade,
Work for all badges and awards,
Work for Jesus Christ our Lord.

Come on lads, don't be afraid
Come and join the Boy's Brigade,
Make new friends, join the squad
Come on in to worship God.

Come on lads, don't be afraid
Come and join the Boy's Brigade
Sign up with our football team
Where winning is our biggest dream.

Janet Abram

Eye of a House

I watch the season's
come and go,
I watch the people,
pass to and fro,
I see most things,
mankind doth miss,
for I am the eye,
of this place,
that I live.

M Livesey

Was it Ten Years Ago

I saw you smile across the street
I hoped it was meant for me
You seemed so nice in your clean cut suit
And I liked what I could see.

I gazed in the window of a shop
Watching your reflection
Then I saw you cross the street
And head in my direction.

'Excuse me, you've dropped your glove'
Your lilting voice said
I turned around and saw your face
Though mine was blushing red
I stammered a gracious 'thank you'
And it was then our eyes met
My feet were rooted to the ground
As I was drawn into your net.

You took my hand in yours
And my toes and fingers curled
But nothing else mattered
Just the two of us in this world.

You swept me off my feet
And I was glad you passed my way
For we fell in love and married
Ten years ago today.

J Gilchrist

My Friends

As a home help
For many years
Days filled with laughter
Other with tears
I loved my friends
Who I did serve
Stories they told
Of bygone times
Dear Wilf who in his youth
Did find
Fighting in the war filled his time
Another a lady
So proud was she
Never thought that I could ever be
Caring and loving
For she did say
You bring such joy to me each day
Your cheerful smile, to say hello
I wait for you, I'm all alone
I listen for your step
The key in my door
They don't realise they give me more
Have you got the time to stay a while
The things they say make me smile
Fill me with wonder, will I ever be as brave
As all my friends
All alone in their by gone days
Waiting and hoping
For someone to call
With open arms to welcome all.

Mona Hardman

Peace

Peace is a lake, on a still still day,
Peace is a calf, asleep on the hay,
Peace is a flower, bursting in bloom,
Peace is a thrush, singing its tune.

Peace is the stillness of falling snow,
Peace is a time, when the breezes blow.
Peace is a moon, lighting the world,
Peace is a star, into universe hurled.

Peace is the darkness drifting away,
Peace is the start of another day.
Peace is the future, stretching ahead,
Peace, I assure you, is when we are dead.

Derek Ashley

11

The Lonely Piper of Glen Shiel

White mists are spread over mountain's tall,
A coverlet for each waterfall.
We wind our way along the Glen,
Pausing as we hear the sound again.

Clad in tartan with Glen Garry hat,
Leather sporran and sheer white spats,
Ruffled shirt, white hose, black shoes,
Kilt a myriad of hues.

Pipes at the shoulder against the light,
Surely a wonderful highland sight.
The lonely piper upon the mound,
Overlooking the windswept sound.

We stand beside the waters verge,
And listen to his mournful dirge,
The lonely piper of Glen Shiel,
Silhouetted upon the hill.

The road to the isles is long ye ken,
So will ye no come back again.
To harken the piper of Glen Shiel,
Haste ye back quick of heel.

F P Lloyd

Disenchanted Wife

I used to dream of my wedding, to a prince, I'd be all in white
He'd be tall and good looking and everything would be great
We'd live in a cottage with roses and a beautiful thatch above
There'd be lots of room for the children and our home would be full
of love.

There'd be a cat, a dog and rabbit, some chickens so we'd have fresh
eggs
The garden as big as a football pitch where rows of white nappies
were pegged
I'd grow all my own herbs and flowers and sew all my cushions and
drapes
There'd be all the free time I wanted whilst he sat there peeling me
grapes

I was sixteen when I first met him, he was slouched on a bar in a vest
He turned and gave me a loving look and I thought 'No God, surely
you jest'
Well he chased me until I had caught him and we wed on a beautiful
day
With me all in white and he looked alright, but his mother caught the
bouquet

The cottage turned into a terrace, the garden? I got a small yard
There was cooking and cleaning and washing on top of a full time
job
Oh, where has the dream of my youth gone! With me as a perfect
mum
I'm lucky to get two bloody minutes after cleaning and changing
their bums

Yes, there's row upon row of white nappies but each one I've had to
scrub
That's after I've cleaned the bath and the loo then it's off to my job in
the pub
Oh where has the prince of my dreams gone where he carries me off
to the moon
I suppose I can dream when I'm sleeping or read of him in Mills and
Boon.

J L Smith

The Menagerie

My house is a menagerie:
Three cats, a dog - and me.

The cats are all neurotic;
They spit and scream and howl.
I watch their crazy antics,
I listen to them yowl.

Bemused, the dog just stares
As they run to and fro;
Although he's big, he would not dare
Upset the status quo.

The cats are small, but vicious:
They keep him in his place.
If he becomes adventurous,
They simply scratch his face.

The killers often leave their trophies
Scattered round the house;
Sometimes you'll find the body
Of a little headless mouse.

The dog's a big black labrador,
Peter is his name.
Sharp white fangs fill his jaw;
This Peter is no saint.

He steals books, and chews them,
But doesn't do much reading;
But he does know how to choose them:
He's got literary breeding.

So you see my home is, in fact,
A wild menagerie;
A big black dog, three crazy cats,
- and then of course there's me.

Paul Smith

Valerie

Like a woodland nymph is she
that lovely girl called Valerie
her dark eyes like pools,
reflections of her many moods,
so bright so gay,
when she is glad,
but oh! how sorry when
she is sad.

Eva Burke

Reminisce of - Some of My Childhood Days

As I sit down, and dream of bygone days
I am back in my childhood once again
The joy of running home to mother
She will have made bread, and lovely barm cakes too
To cut in slices whilst warm,
And spread with butter,
And raspberry jam too
That was our joy, and delight after school

We each of us had our special jobs to do
But we were so happy, and contented too
The days seemed so long, that they would never end
But oh, the joy to be living just then
There was always time to stop and chat with a friend
That meant more to me,
Than silver or gold.

We was blessed with pastures to explore
The clumps of violets, down the side of the ditches,
And the lovely golden faces of the marigold
The cowslip, ladies slipper, cuckoo flower, and daisies too
And lots more, and beautiful grasses too
The song of the thrush, blackbird, robin and others
And all this beauty is for us to see
And I thank God for his wonderful world.

M A Topping

Untitled

Sadly stands the empty swing,
A lonely and neglected thing.
Where are the toys, there yesterday
They now have all been put away.

The leaves are falling, crisp and brown
And dandelion clocks drift down.
Little feet are heard no more
On paths where they once trod before.

Little pegs on little line
No longer are put out with mine.
What happened to our happy hours?
Gone like summer's dying flowers.

Autumn's here and days grow cool
My little one has started school.

Joyce Williams

Be Careful

Be careful - he loves you now
As only he knows how
I remember when he loved me too
But left, to live with you.
Your light burns bright for him - for now
His fickle heart is yours - but how
Long before he tires of you and stirs
Himself to leave, and live with her?
Be careful - he loves you now.

J Watson

Memories

There is a place I know so well
It's name is memory lane
I like to visit there sometimes
To meet my friends again
And as I take those magic steps
Along that treasured mile
I hear the laughter ringing there
And I linger there awhile
The folks I meet aren't rich or grand
They're honest and they're kind
I feel the warmth of their embrace
And clasp each trusting hand
We sit and talk of bygone days
How friendship stood the test
We shared the joys we shared the tears
And always did our best
I know they say the past is gone
And we must go our way
But there would be no present
I f there were no yesterday
For memories are precious things
Which we can always borrow
They give us strength to carry on
And hope for each tomorrow
And so I'll keep that secret key
That opens memory lane
And when a day looks dreary
I'll visit there again.

Lilian Gore

The First Aid Examination

Doctor, just before we begin this first aid examination
Could I tell you about my problem, and ask for your co-operation
To improve my knowledge and practical skills, ever is my intention
But I suffer mental incontinence, when I most need a memory
retention

I can answer the questions others are asked and with greater fluency
too
But as soon as it's my turn to answer, I usually haven't a clue
With grazes, puncture and sucking wounds, lacerated, incised, and
contused
Gunshot, crush and blast injuries, It's no wonder that I'm confused

What can you tell me, I am asked, about the treatment for shock
Hysteria, asthma, or welders flash, the answer is - not a lot
Then I'm asked about foreign bodies, hernias, cramp and migraine
When I would prefer the questions on hypothermia, burns or a sprain

The treatment for suspected fractures is total immobilization
That's easy to say but hard to do when you've just lost you
co-ordination
An unconscious casualty who can be moved should be placed in
recovery fast
I can do that with the greatest of ease, the trouble is I'm never asked

Abdominal pain or injury and emergency childbirth I know
But glycaemia gives me some problems, as I mix up hyper with
hypo
When It comes to poisons or snake bites, I'm out of my depth I'm
afraid
I give nil by mouth, have a brandy myself, and send for medical aid

On heart attacks and convulsions I can always find something to say
And I'm fully aware that compression can look like a cva
I'm not incompetent really, I honestly try my best
It's just in examinations that I'm not as good as the rest

I'm not asking for any favours, but it would help a little bit
If you asked me about the things I know, then I wouldn't look so
                                                                    thick
To conclude may I say thank-you in hopeful anticipation
Of getting enough marks to pass this first aid examination.

Sandra E Ronson

Sunday with Gran

It's Sunday and we are going to grans
She cooks a dinner better than mam's
I love her roasters and Yorkshire pud
She gives me pickles if I've been good
The best thing of all, if I eat it all gone
She lets me wash up with her pinny on
Apple pie, ice cream and scones with jam
Oh I do love Sundays with my gran.

Jo Clemo

Garden in Winter

Under the oak tree
The rain gathers in a grey mist;
Delicate beads of glass waver
On the thorns of the quick-set hedge
Till they drop
Onto the rain-bright leaves below.

A robin, like a tiny flame,
Darts from the fence, to forage
Among the Autumn-fallen leaves,
And the skull-like cabbages
Left from the Summer crop.

Gone are the Summer sounds:
The blaring transistors, the shouting children,
The chattering women.
Gone is the Summer pageant:
The flaring roses,
The purple-trumpeting petunias,
The soaring blue-spired delphiniums.

The garden is grey and silent,
Submitting to the onslaught of the rain;
Biding her time
Till Spring shall rescue her again.

M U Johnson

The Ancient City

This land of plenty, I loved so much;
I still see the mansions towering high.
A thousand windows I reach to touch
And gaze at the dome, up to the sky.

The streets which meander here and there.
Ancient carts drawn by oxen strong,
Beggars sit and hope someone will care,
And drop them a coin - they wait so long.

The rich have no time for this fated band
And toss them aside as vermin stale,
While they feed off the fat of the land
As they listen to their jester's tale.

Life is pleasant for the rich and free,
But a cruel place for beggar and such;
'Tis not bulk which makes man better be,
The lowly slave measures twice as much.

But pomp and vanity all must fall;
The mighty have despair as they feel
Their world begins to crumble - and call -
Too late - no one hears their sad appeal.

The earth begins to tremble and moan,
Temples shatter and sink 'neath the sand.
Nothing remains - just a scream - a groan,
Lifeless things upon an ancient land.

Half sunk pillars like marble fingers
Reaching out to covet the green grass,
As the warming breeze gently lingers,
To kiss every blade and then to pass.
Marjorie J M Eardley

Old Jane's Corner Shop

I recall as a child, I often would pause,
Anticipating with joy-filled glee,
The wondrous delights - an aladdins cave,
That awaited, behind the door, for me.

From potatoes and peas and tins of meat,
To candles and 'brasso' and balls of string.
Rainbow kali, only tuppence an ounce!
The corner shop sold 'most everything!

An apple brown face, and a cheery smile,
Old Jane had a greeting for all,
Men and women, young and old,
Always knew they were welcome to call.

A timeless quality existed there,
Amongst the many items sold,
Life, love and hope all met together,
Scandals and secrets, never retold.

I often wonder today as I shop,
In modern times, how Jane would have fared,
The supermarkets, so impersonal and cold,
Wouldn't be room for someone who cared.

Gillian Cookson

Haunted

Your love is like a friendly ghost,
You can't touch it, and you can't always see it,
But you somehow know that it is always there,
Watching over me,
And it won't hurt me, unless I hurt it first,
I am haunted by your love, yet feel totally at peace,
I now hope that your love, is finally laid to rest, we can rest in each
                                                                  other.
When I'm sleeping I know your love will keep me safe from hurtful
                                                              images

Your love is full, yet ever growing
I've been blessed with your love, and compassion

Please haunt me, forever...

L Steadman

The Stag Night

The morning after, the night before,
Staggering round, in his undies and socks.
His head feels like, a lump of lead,
And his belly, full of rocks.

Got to get, a move on fast,
Must be at the church, by nine.
A face in the mirror, with sunken eyes,
Looks out, 'oh God', he says, 'it's mine.

'Got any alka seltzer mum?'
He asks, full of self pity.
Splashing his face with water, thinks,
My eyes don't half feel gritty.

Last nights stag do, was a wow,
A pub crawl, on the town.
Smoking pot, he was high as a kite,
Not worried about, the come down.

Too much booze, his head is banging,
Oh what a sorry sight.
Who was that, he was dancing with,
And made a date with, for tonight?

He vaguely remembered, the strippers,
With whom he danced, the seven veils.
But what he did with the bunny girl,
Alas his memory fails.

Heaven knows, how he got home,
At seven am, off his head.
He puts his shoes, inside the fridge,
And the milk, under his bed.

Now the taxi's at the door,
Last check, yes you got the ring.
Wishing he could just, go up to bed,
And forget the whole damned thing.

Mother's head shakes, in disgust,
Saying, 'take off that look of gloom.
You're only standing as best man.
Thank God you're not the groom.'

Madeline Kavanagh

Fly, Eagle, Fly

Fly, eagle, fly
So swift and fearless on the wing,
In striking grace you rule the sky
Where you alone are king;
And I below gaze with delight
And fascination at your flight.

Fly, eagle, fly
There's none to challenge or to harm
you in the sky. I watch you ply
your aerial kingdom, clear and calm;
You eyes see everything below,
They follow me wherever I go.

Fly, eagle, fly
Stay clear of man's ingenious snares,
Avoid them well, or you'll die.
Man seeks to harm you for he fears,
Unlike you, he will never be
As swift and fearless and as free.

Fly, eagle, fly
Make for lofty mountain-side,
Where man will never dare to try
In vain to boost his battered pride.
To reach you, he must climb as high.
To catch you, he is sure to die.

James C Thomas

A Northern Town

A sweet smell of mown grass pervaded the air,
Cattle grazed lazily atop a hill where
I stood looking down on a small Northern town...
Across chimneys tall, now blackened with soot,
Their silence now eerie... no more the hoot
Of a whistle at close of day,
When workers foot weary plodded their way
Home from the toil of a dusty day.

I fancied I heard the crash of a loom
The rattle of a tram along the track... its boom
Causing sparks to fill the air
As it came into contact with overhead cables there.
The streets... once alive with hurrying clogged feet
Are deserted right now from morning till night.

'Mark my words' I can hear my father say
'The firing of rockets will cause trouble someday,
It's not reet to disturb all yon beauty above...
It was put theer by God... for us all to love',
I stood looking down on my Northern town...
And I sigh...

Jenny Horrocks

You are my Friend...

Far away across the miles
each day I think of you,
when I'm feeling up or down
happy, sad or blue.

It doesn't matter what the mood
I am in at the time,
we always seem to have a chat
completely in the mind.

It's either in the kitchen
or lunching in the town,
drinking coffee all day long -
oblivious of what's around.

The best of gifts that I have
which you have given me -
is to have a friend like you;
it means so much to me.

You really are the best of friends
that anyone could wish,
I thank you on this Mother's Day -
you are a special gift.

J L Lloyd

A Memory of a Prayer

This child that I watch, kneels to pray,
This child that I saw yesterday.
A tear rolls slowly down that sad little face,
So innocent and young, it leaves a wet trace.

She calls up to Heaven with a voice unheard?
Does God hear her every word?
She looks up to Heaven, her eyes appealing,
They close in anguish as her gaze meets the ceiling.

She is praying so hard for something inside,
Two more tears as I kneel down beside.
She does not see me, she is lost in a daze,
Lost in her prayer, in Heavens haze.

The child slips away in this now foggy room,
And this church becomes quite empty soon.
Lost in time, I travel through space,
That child has grown up and left no trace.

Only a memory of a prayer unheard,
It seems God never listened to a single word,
For the prayer went unanswered, I know, you see,
For the child in my memory, I know, was me.

Margaret Caldwell

34

Deane Road Kids

Down Deane road where I was born and lived for many years
In an atmosphere of factory smoke
Of laughter and of tears
Money was scarce but we still had fun
We made our own you see
Beneath the street lamp we would sit and dream of what would be
Cath would be an air hostess and travel to foreign parts
Jean would be a film star and break a million hearts
As for me my love was music so on the stage I'd go
My singing and tap dancing would set the world aglow
But alas it seemed t'was not to be
It didn't work that way
Cath and Jean worked in the mill and toiled for little pay
I went to be a sales girl - a far cry from the stage
But Saturday nights I sang in clubs to complement my wage
The years rolled on and so did we
To go our separate ways
But still I keep the memory strong of those happy childhood days
Deane road's still there
But the shops have gone
Yet in my memory
I recall the Regent picture house and the queues for the matinees
The Windmill pub and Butler's pies
The old tank temperance shop
Where we listened to the juke box playing trad jazz and be-hop
Those days have gone
But I still think of the zany things we did
In years gone by when I was young and just a Deane road kid.

Doreen Smith

Talk to Them

The rose, I behold you so perfectly formed
Such beauty and scent to bloom forth from the ground
In your scarlet red gown you're a token of love
And when you wear your jewels of dewdrops
Which descend from above
Your beauty enhanced can only be matched
By your sisters galore, bordering my patch
In their colours and hues of pink, yellow and white
To be queen of the flowers is your well deserved right.

Margaret E Hampson

Late Party

We stayed to see the break of day
And early morning sunlight.
We lingered on the homeward way,
Not long since bathed in moonlight.

Our heads moved closer, just we two,
Alone in Nature's keeping.
And for a period, time, we knew,
Had stayed his ceaseless reaping.

J P R Vernon

Futile

I am back stretcher bearer - the one facing you.
On a branchless, leafless shrub - next to a pond
Overflowing with crimson liquid - someone had attached
an epitaph 'Soldiers taking a blood bath.'
I think as I help to carry him, 'Christmas Day yesterday.
Truce! No stretchers. No casualties. Today?
This is the first. He's light as lavender.
A fledgling soldier. A lad - Taffy.
Pulped into a red jelly, spiked with splintered bones
Like yesterday's trifle.
Last night we had sat with the enemy beneath the stars.
They listened while we Christians sang 'Holy Night'.
Taffy told us about his mining village. The Wesleyan Chapel.
Choir practice. A girl at the Grammar School - Julie.
Black-haired, rounded, ripe!
On too high a tree for him to touch.
But one day he'd promised himself, he'd reach her.
Night school. Perhaps, even the Open University.
The coal dust was already a sitting tenant in his black lungs.
We'd heard him coughing and rattling in the small hours.
Rattles and guns pea-souped together.
At seventeen, Julie had married the local doctor.
Too soon for him to reach her. The mine had closed.
No jobs anywhere. Moved to Cardiff. Nothing there either.
Trekked up to Manchester. He wouldn't tell us what happened there.
Tight-lipped. 'Change the subject, lads!'
When we went through his effects - not much. One letter.
On the flap - 'From another knight of the road, second bench.
To Sam, third bench, Piccadilly Gardens, Manchester.'
'Goodnight, Taffy, in the blighted morning of your life.
You'll meet the Governor first. Say one for us. Oh God!
It's urgent. Say it now. Quick. Here's another Scud with an anthrax
head. Don't bother, Taffy, it's futile.

Doris Kirby

I Remember

Memories are treasured things,
Like puppy dogs and dragon fly wings.
Kisses that linger on the lips
Thoughts that last, like sails on ships.
Babies playing on the floor,
Children peeping round the door,
Laughs and giggles and other sounds
That stay forever, I'll be bound.
Remembrances of folk long gone,
Fathers, mothers, daughters, sons.
All were here and lived their lives,
We can gain from their many vibes.
The world is a wondrous place
Where we can live and grow apace
And learn and teach as we go on,
Just pass the message to your son.
Your daughters too will benefit
From wisdom you may care to give.
So my friends as life we bear,
Just remember to be fair
And just in all you do,
The world will help you see it through.

Peg Holman

The Curate's Wife

Am I searching for a God
Or am I just a lousy sod?
As slowly up the aisle I go
To where the candles softly glow
Glowing on the Communion cup
From which we sinners all must sup
Are others hypocrites like me
Who from the devil try to flee
Or are they saints upon this earth
Amusing God with songs of mirth?

Drusilla West

The Golden Girls

We are Olive, Winnie, Madge and Ann,
Four of us widows without a man,
But life goes on, so we do the best we can,
Its like bread and butter, but without the jam.

So off on holiday we all do go.
We walk and we talk, and we dance if there's a floor,
And tho' we're getting older we're not prepared to go,
So we carry on regardless sometimes fast and sometimes slow.

And when we do get home, its good to close our own front door
Tho' there's no one there to meet us and greet us (hi, hello)
But we hope they're up in heaven gazing down on us below
And you can almost hear them whisper,
(Keep it up girls, have a go).

Madge Smith

'Just Thinkin'
To all Writers Everywhere!

It's ner' as hard as you might think,
To put a few words together.
There's alus' summat to talk about.
Folks, an o' course the weather!
Ya' can go on an' on an' on an' on.
Ner' get tired o' writin'!
There's alus' somethin' to talk about.
If it's only the bairns that's fighting'!
A few sweet verse, short and terse.
Pen in ma' hand and ma' wit.
It's a wee bit a' fun that a' really enjoy.
An' a really love to do it!
So if days are too long.
An' you've naught else ta' do,
An' ya' weary of ole' Father time.
Then get thee a pen.
An' get thee a pad.
An' write thee a wee bit o'rhyme!

Kick Off Time!

Our lady in waiting, draped on her couch
Is dreaming down the days.
She ponders, and espies her lively pouch
Practising footballing ways;
Or maybe 'tis Prima trying her points
With ballet in her toes.
Whatever it is that's flexing its joints
'Twill be needing strong 'Babygrows'!
Enjoy the encumbrance of the next generation,
A miniature now, but perfect.
'Twill be magic indeed, your joint procreation,
A new life, of wonder, of prospect.

Jennifer Wright

Colourful Year

Tinsell-silvered white - when words take shape in hoary air,
Blanketed landscapes broken by blacks and greys,
Skies clear as sight, star-filled in moonlights glare,
No boundary edging green from blue on snow filled Winters days.

Green is the colour of re-birth, but when does birth begin?
With new fruit peering coyly from the womb wherein they lay?
Or bleached lamblets and home-building birds with tuneful din?
Or the heady air of promise that says Spring is on its way?

Endless golden days, short nights with purple hues,
Blood red mottled twilights and blue dragon flies at play,
Speckled fish angling for insects on silver plated pools,
And perfumed pollen colouring all the summer sun-kissed rays.

Brown is the shade of sleep after summer has gone,
Orange, ochre, amber too, in the leafy paved ways,
Of Hazel coloured forests who sleep now the blossoms done,
Painting canvases of copper as autumn makes its play.

John Burton

My House

Worn out pillow that's going back years
Torn up quilt that holds many tears
Thing on the sideboard you know
I think it's called a radio
Dad comes up whistling a song
Then he say's 'Anything wrong'
I say 'No' he says 'go to sleep'
So I close my eyes without a peep
In the morning mum says you look a disgrace
Go back upstairs and wash your face
I walk upstairs as quiet as a mouse
I wish I lived in a nicer House.

Julie Wright

45

Nicki

I want to help, I really do
Put your life together.
To shelter you from all life's storms
Like a great big umbrella
But you have flown the nest my child
You're out there on your own
The great big world just whispered
Come on, it's time, you've grown.
So the haven of your early years
Was quickly cast aside
As you ventured out into the night
For a rough and stormy ride
But if it ever gets too tough
Or you feel you need a friend
Someone to care, or just be there
A listening ear to lend
Remember the king in a castle called home
He'd give you the moon no less
Or put the stars in the night to set the world right
For you his little princess

Shirley Ann Slater

To a Friend

When there was trouble in my life,
I was feeling sad and blue.
You would always be around
To help me make it through.

I felt my life was at an end
I had lost all strength and hope.
You were there to talk it through
Helping me to cope.

When I was afraid and nothing seemed,
To help me calm my fears.
Your shoulder it was always there,
So I could shed my tears.

You helped retain my sanity
On you I could depend.
So for all these things and many more
I deeply thankyou. Friend!

Pauline Case

After Twenty Eight Years (or 25/4/87)

Will anyone remember me a hundred years today?
Will anybody care about my life,
Or give a second thought to if I laughed or if I cried,
Or care about what I perceive as strife?

No-one will remember that I sat upon this bench
In the Churchyard, on the hill above Hawkshead,
Or the picture of the sun upon the hills and on the lake,
Forever locked away inside my head.

When the scene has been completed and the canvas left to dry
And the picture hung for those who wish to see,
Will anybody notice all the blemishes and marks
That seem to cause so much concern to me?

Will it matter if I drove the biggest car or if I walked,
Or left a million pounds or not a dime,
Or owned a country mansion or settled in a tent,
Or left for somewhere late or spot on time?

Will people stop and look at all that's happened in my life
And say, 'There must have lived a happy man.
If only I'd had half the happy times he fell upon!'
Which goes to show, Enjoy it while you can.

Why worry all about the downward slopes we sometimes hit!
Without them, all the highs would seem demure
And what are now the lofty heights would then appear the lows
Which then we'd wonder how we could endure.

I only have this moment once, to use to best effect
And only now can I enjoy it live.
What a waste to only recognise the good in retrospect.
The greatest joy is that you now derive.
A J Rayner

All God's Gifts Around Us?

I held a flower in my hand and marvelled at its intricate beauty,
A tiny miracle of creation, so perfect, so pure,
But its dewy softness reminded me of the tender bloom of her skin
That I can no longer touch.

I watched a glistening pearl drop of summer dew sparkling on the
grass,
Fresh and glowing and new,
But it reminded me of the silent tear that rested on her lashes
When she was too weak to cry.

A butterfly danced by, light as air and full of joy,
I was entranced by its free spirit and winsome ways,
But its fragile delicacy reminded me of the transience of her life
So vibrant, so colourful, so easily destroyed.

The night sky twinkled with a million stars
Each one a tiny jewel to be treasured,
But they reminded me of how her love shone out and how precious
she was,
And how unattainable and and far away she is now.

I felt a lazy breeze that stirred the autumn leaves
Like a warm caress across my face,
But it reminded me of her gentle kiss goodbye
And the hush of her last breath.

There is no solace to be found in the wonder and beauty of nature for
me.
Or in the glory and love of God's creation
It all only serves to remind me of the glory and the beauty,
The wonder and the warmth,
The love and the loving,
That I have lost.
Marilyn Shawe

Untitled

Tread softly o'er their graves.
Lest we should wake the sleeping dead
They slumber on and know not that we are overhead.

O M Thomas

Daydream

If a poem paints a picture
In shades of jaded green.
I'll sit and write a poem
That will idolise this scene,
To sing to you of beauty
That you'll seek but never find.
For the poem that I'm writing is a picture in my mind.

I'm sat upon a hilltop
Where the birds about me fly,
With jollity and freedom in a vivid sapphire sky.
Caressed by graceful cotton clouds
That are my boundless friends.
Sailing through the endless air
Until my vision ends.

R Horrocks

I am

Sometimes under downcast skies
I gaze with prejudicial eyes.
I look around and all I see
Is people looking back at me.
I look at them, they look at me,
I look again and all I see
Is people looking back at me.

They have no right at me to stare
Or cast that patronising glare,
Or ever hope to re-arrange
Or ever hope my life to change.
For I feel envy grief, sadness, joy,
I feel relief and sometimes coy.
I feel the breeze and often rain.
I've witnessed love and witnessed pain.
I've seen the sun both rise and set,
And with life and death I have met.

So sit upon your righteous chair
But save that patronising glare,
Though you may think you'll never be
Any kinder, wiser or richer than me
And if you were, I would not change
Or ever wish to re-arrange,
For I am what I am and always will be
Regardless of what another may see,
Regardless of what another may know.
I am what I am and will always be so.

Joyce Nisbet

Untitled

When God made the World
He said with a smile
Here! it's all yours
I'll rest for a while
and what have we done
with his wonderful gift

Robbed the rainforests
of millions of trees
Polluted the air
The rivers, the seas.

And where will it end
you may very well ask
for somebody, someday
will inherit a task

So why don't we start
with might and with main
to make this old Planet
a clean one again

For the sake of our Children
and their Children too
I think we should
How about you.

M Neville-Cooke

The Bottle

It's another night and Eloise sits all alone again.
Staring at an empty bottle, she silently weaps.
No-body hears her, no-body comes near her.
The quiet embers die away
she wishes she could too.

Time has no meaning, days come and days go.
She allows herself just one special friend,
Who listens quietly and gives comfort to her.
A warm comfort, but all too soon
that disappears too.

So Eloise will make a new friend when she shops again
A new bottle to talk to, just someone to listen.
She hears bottles rattling together now.
And realises its the milkman, she's
talked herself into another lonely day.

S Marshall

Softly Sleeps

The moon and clouds raced the sky.
Thor in his eternal parade charged past the stars.
The stars, dimmed occasionally by cracks of light.
Brilliant white light.
But cold and frightening.

The privacies invaded by thunder bold
Electric energy of lightening leaps.
But put that aside and sit and hold,
My little one while she softly sleeps.

On and on, the storm grows stronger
While softly, softly still she sleeps.
On and on, the night lasts longer
While softly, softly still she sleeps.

Blue skies are at sunrise
Still I watch my little one
For her blue eyes are yet unwise
Un-opened to the deeds that men have done.

Kathryn Anderton

Time

Time shall free mind and soul
And heal the wounded heart
Giving faith and hope again
Where grief hath torn apart

Time is true as steel itself
Waiting to console
Giving strength where needed most
Lightning the toll

Time is healing through the pain
Yet pain is hard to bear
Invisibly mending ...
Banishing all care

Time is but a mirage to some
A light they cannot see
But it will strike like lightning
Hence ... grieving shall cease to be.

Enid Harrison

Rainfall

Put up no parasols against the gentle rain
For Gods tears from Heaven fall to wash away the pain
Your pain and my pain as all around we see
Mounds of devastation caused by you and me.
Destruction from the greedy heart, the eye in search of gain
The one with ever ready hand to grasp the seeds of grain.

Fall gentle rain and wash away the sin,
The sin of man's hypocrisy and races he won't win
Lay down your arms and open up your ears
And hear the winds of Heaven rustle in the breeze.
For future generations will gather in the wold
To feed the mouths of poverty and mine the plastic gold.

Let the gentle rainfall increase the harvest, then
Wash away the hunger and the sins of mortal men.

Jean Carroll

To Michael
(My Valentine Wish for you)

Who made the water flow down from the mountain to the stream?
Who put the stars in the dark night sky, to twinkle and to gleam?
Who made the grass so lush and green, and corn such a golden hue?
Who made the poppy head so red and the summer sky so blue?
If I could wish a life for you I would pray that you would find
A store of God's finest treasure and simplicity of mind
To see, to hear, to smell, to touch, a soul of deep concern
For you to know that I love you, oh! so much
And for you to love me deeply in return.

V M Clegg

The Ark

The animals went in two by two,
Noah saved them all,
Every creature upon the earth,
Whether winged, big or small.

Stormy times have now returned,
Born of ignorance and greed,
An ark is just not large enough,
To protect all those in need.

The damage done by humankind,
Is shameful and so vast,
We surely must put right again.
Mistakes made in the past.

Nature gives to us the answers,
And animals show the way,
The time has come to listen,
And follow what they say.

We must learn peace and harmony,
If our earth is to survive,
And treasure God's creation,
If we wish to stay alive.

Susan Ashley Middleton

Proverbs

They are, like nuts, each in a shell,
Crisp, compact, bouncy, crackable,
Long - lasting, passed from mouth, by ears,
To mouth again. I wonder where
Or when, the first mouth spoke,
The first ears heard, the first minds took
Up the meaning, chewed upon it
Like gum, year after year, through cold and heat,
Hard luck and smooth. Tumbled in
The mill of life they wear to roundness;
Squeezed to oil, help wheels to turn,
Impart a sheen, a gleam of soundness.
They balance, like a juggler's balls,
They fight in fun; we tell them they are false
But they bound back, these chips of truth,
Splinters of God's image, husks of faith.

Gordon Read

60

Mental Block

I suppose I knew it would happen
This lack of inspiration
I try to pour out my thoughts
But I only pour out perspiration

It's odd to think I'm sweating
When I'm complaining of drying up
I'm all washed out, yet really
There's nothing left in my cup

I'd like to write more poems
But the rhymes are no longer there
I've bitten my nails to the elbows
And pulled out all of my hair

But I suppose I should hang up my pen
And call it a premature end
I shall continue to be a policeman
'Til I've completely gone round the bend

If only I could find more rhymes
To slacken this writer's noose
Even an articulate alliteration
But no, it's just no use.

Stuart A McIntosh

Courage

It takes courage to see something through
When all you want to do is run away
Stand your ground then you shall have courage
It is hard I know when you are
A coward at heart
If you find the will and the way
Your courage comes to stay

O Harnby

March

Were you awakened through the night
By a vicious howling roar,
That rattled chimney pots and slates
And threatened to break the door?

I dreamed of lairs by jungle pools
Where wild beasts quench their thirst,
Then, wakening, I remembered,
To-day is March the first.

The month that comes in like a lion
With tawny mane high flying,
Then, frolicking, frisking, like a lamb,
It leaves in soft winds sighing.

The frosty air will nip the buds,
And make the spring flowers shiver,
While gale force winds tear through the vale,
And solid oak trees quiver.

Each day we see an earlier dawn,
And warmer grows the sun,
Till day and night are equal
When the calender reads twenty-one.

'Tis then we see the calmer days
When softer winds caress the trees,
The frozen earth, with grip relaxed,
Responding to the gentler breeze.

Then let us sing 'In praise of Spring',
Our thankfulness expressing,
Rejoicing in the verdant scene,
That yields so rich a blessing.
Clifford Daniels

Hunted

There she stood, magnificent!
Her big brown soft eyes glittering in the sunlight,
The leaves swaying gently behind her!
I think she knew where I stood, and why!
I raised the barrel of my gun, slowly
until it was positioned,
She raised her gallant head, nostrils flaring, inhaling deeply,
She knew I was there and why!

I knew if I didn't shoot now,
I would lose her,
The gun went off with a sickening bang,
Thrusting my shoulder back with the force,

She seemed to hit the moss gracefully,
and when the smoke cleared,
There she lay, lifeless.

Then out of the silence, came a faint crack,
The crack of a twig,
Stunned as I watched a helpless, tiny fawn, emerge from the under·
                                                    growth.

There she stood, uneasily sniffing the air,
tentative steps, the new smell of death,
I think she knew where I stood and why,
then!
bang.

Kate Ashmore

Him to Her

Hearts tearing through day and night,
Losing all the will to fight.
Not a single moment passing by,
When all I want to do is cry.

Need the strength to see this through,
Soon, to be just me and you.
Was I right, was I wrong,
Still don't know how to hold my tongue.

Past, Present, Future, all rolled into one,
Do I have the power to carry this one on.
Stupid, stupid, stupid me,
When will I learn what I have to be.

But what am I to any-one?
Your love is lost, our friendship gone.
Do you recognise my cry for help,
With all life's problems I have been dealt.

Please let me into your life again,
Never meant to cause you all this pain.
My love for you will never cease,
All I'm saying is please, please, please!

Sarah-Jane Hunter

Fairie Tale

There was a tale a long time ago,
It tells of fairies and how they grow.
They start as special thoughts you see,
From ordinary people like you and me.

Then the magic will only come right,
On a dark and starry night.
A wishing star gets plucked from the dark,
And looked at for a wishing mark.

A butterfly is caught in a fine mesh net,
They are put together, the spell is set.
The spell goes to another land,
Where mother nature puts in her hand.

She feeds them all with magic dust,
To be a good fairie, it is a must.
And so the fairie goes to school,
To learn what's right, she is no fool.

Linda Robinson

Created they Seven

Sunday is Sols day
Creator of light
Birch is their leader
And Lucifer slights

Monday is Lunas day
Creator of the seas
Willow is her wisdom
Mammon and Avarice at ease

Tuesday belongs to Mars
Master of land and trees
Holly his holy sprig
Asmodeus laughs with glee

Wednesday is Odins
His the seasons and stars
His spear is made from Ash
Angry Satan marrs

Thor is Thursday
Sea beast and birds he rules
And his tree is the oak
Strange Beelzebub fools

Our Goddess Freia owns Friday
Creatrix of beast and man
The apple of life her fruit
Leviation her serpent spans

Saturn in Saturday
He rests at ease all day
Alder tree his stake
Bran his twin is away
M J Pallister

Our Parents

They are always willing
To do the best for us,
They do it in a cheerful mood
And Never make a fuss.

They help us when we're worried
And when we're tired and ill.
They're cross when we are naughty
But they always love us still.

And so when they are aged
And we are still quite young,
We must help our parents
Who, so much for us have done.

M Williams

A Boy

A boy is a creature, so complex inside,
With feelings that flow in and out, like the tide,
One minute he's loving, the next he's a brat,
But you can't help but love him, despite all of that!

He can whistle and sing, drive you mad with his noise
He never is tidy, a roomful of toys,
His comics are strewn on the floor - (as of leaves),
And a home win for Liverpool's part of his dreams.

He flies round the house, like the eye of a storm,
His energy's boundless, well that's quite the norm,
But if there's an errand or task to be done,
He's off like a shot - with - 'I won't be long, Mum'!

He's deaf when it suits him - (but nosey as well).
He hears things he shouldn't. (You hope he won't tell!),
He loves Mutant Turtles, computers and bikes,
He's not keen on bathing or homework at nights.

He loves radio one, watches 'Top of the Pops',
His chatter is constant - the noise never stops,
But when it's Mum's birthday - he really is proud,
Of the card and the present he's bought you from Town.

His world is quite small - for a few years or so,
But his endless enquiries will help it to grow,
I look at his face, filled with innocence yet,
And I see there the man, that a sweetheart will get.

He's tough and he's noisy - untidy as well,
He's loving and naughty and argues as well,
He's all of these things which are rolled into one,
But, for all that, I love him, for he is my son.
Joan Wheeler

My Love

I trampled all the pastures
I doved the flesh with mail
My helmet flashed its steelness
And my heart began to pale
My sword was living lightning
My breastplate was my thought
My duty was my palanquin
Love flowed to Heaven thus bought
I journeyed past the stars
Milk was all vermilion
Honey was my delight
My silence was a galleon:
The Eternal held His living breath
And vomited the pleasure
Of my sin to instant death:
My love she spoke so tenderly
And grief was in her eye
But we never spoke nor looked at each
Nor ever wondered why.

G H Gregory

The Ageless Trees

Life is but a short, swift, span,
Not so for the trees
green, then bare, then new shoots come
and open by degrees.

In the meadows, open wide,
through the forests side by side
down the hilly slopes they slide
living on forever.

How many trees have seen how many wars?
strong, ageless and undaunting
waving in the summer breeze
then menacing and haunting
In the spring a new life starts
bringing joy and beauty
We die and everything is gone
They fulfil their duty.

Veronica Ryder

Inside Out

I don't want to go
They can't make me
I don't want to go
They try to take me
This place is mine
Not theirs
I'm fighting to stay
Who cares
Don't let them here
I don't want to go
They fill me with fear
Yet I'm burning to know
Who are *they?*
And why have they come
Send them away
To wherever they're from
I can't live there
They can't live here
But it's them who will dare
And me who will fear
If I let myself go
I'm taking a chance
To say goodbye
No second glance
Then I'll be gone
And they will be me
We are all one
But I won't see.

Lesley Goodall

The People Don't Care

On the edge of the park
she stands alone -
no family, no friends
no permanent home

She begs for money
in the street,
and rummages in dustbins
for something to eat

She has no credit
to her name,
she lives in fear
lives in shame

The people don't care
she thinks, she knows
nobody cares -
which way it goes

What would her mother
to her now say?
her beloved daughter
who dreads each new day.

Matthew Weir

73

Hold me Gently

Do not hold me tight,
give me room,
let me take flight,
day or night.

Let me see salmon leap,
or let me sleep,
let me see fields of green,
and golden corn,
at early dawn,
let me see mountains tall
or else, I fall.
be kind, these are pictures
in my mind,
when I'm all alone,
and my mind takes flight,
release me,
don't hold me tight.

Margaret Hornby

To John - Born on January 20th 1983

Today a dream has been fulfilled,
And all our hearts with gladness filled.
What sheer delight - what happy joy!
O welcome! Welcome! Little boy!

Dear tiny babe, the love you bring,
Eclipses every other thing.
God's gracious gift - they'll call you John.
O welcome! Welcome! Little son!

May you be happy all life through
And find success in all you do,
Your days content - your ways be glad.
O Welcome! Welcome! Bonny lad!

J Burnell

Counting my Losses

When will I see through these very dark skies
When will the veil lift off my eyes
How can I temper my doubts and fears
And find an answer for all the years I've squandered and
thrown away

The good times I've had, the money I've wasted the honey
and wine and love I've tasted
The disappointment I feel when I look around
And see lesser men, with a larger pound
And think you silly, stupid, experienced fool

Edward Ellis Doyle

Mondays

Monday wash day shop day
Back to work day after a sunny weekend
Back to the old routine get the kids off to school.
'Mummy I don't want to go! Can't we
stay home and play?
You must be joking its Monday!

J Ottey

Three Little Curious Cats

Three little curious curious cats
Inside boxes, under hats
Up the curtains
On the chairs
Clawing carpets - need repairs

Three little curious curious cats
Hanging upside down like bats
Never tiring
Never still
Moments with adventure fill

Three little curious curious cats
Chasing after absent rats
In the garden
Up the tree
Hide and seek's more fun with three

Three little curious curious cats
Lying on the fireside mats
Busy day
Tired out now
Curious cats ... Goodnight .... Miaow!

P Paterson

Untitled

At the end of the day when you're weary
It's very hard to keep cheery,
But if you remember when you smile
It's as if the sun shines for a while
A smile spreads warmth to others
It's such a pity no one bothers
Sometimes making new friends
Only on your smile depends.
Notice when you go to town
How many folk wear a frown
We all have problems I am sure
Most of them a smile could cure
The world could be a happier place
If we put on a cheerful face
We'd have less wrinkles on our brow
Even look younger than we do now

Audrey Steventon

79

Whit-Week Walk

The drab grey street in Lowry Land
Was lazing on a Sabbath morn
When from afar was heard a band,
And into life the street was born.

At the street end, the children peered
Excitedly towards the sounds,
A throng of people had appeared,
The Church flock walked the Parish bounds.

The slow process led by the band,
Whose instruments gleamed silver bright,
Produced a steady rhythm, grand
Sound to match the moving sight.

The Sunday Scholars all wore blue.
Each girl in pastel colour dressed.
The boys wore suits of darker hue
With knife edged creases, neatly pressed.

The Church's Banner held on high,
By Youths in their 'Fraternity',
Brightened up a dull grey sky.
Proclaimed to all their Faith to see.

The Rector, curates, choirboys too,
In snow-white surplices arrayed,
Sang Hymns of praise as they passed through.
The dignitaries of this parade.

An old man had surveyed the scene,
(Procession over, pageant gone),
On his pad sketched what had been
In Lowry Land this dull grey morn.
John Dibble

Rachel

My name is Rachel, and I am sixty three.
Doesn't anyone give a damn about me.
They want to put me in a tiny flat,
Three floors up, Now! fancy that.
Just throw the old crone up in the sky,
forget about her until she dies.
Though Rheumatism and Arthritis rack my bones
there's no-one around to hear my groans.
A bungalow or cottage on the ground,
Now to me my dears, that would be sound.
With roses and shrubs in front of the door,
Instead of stuck up here, on the third floor,
I am an old woman with very few needs,
Won't somebody, somewhere, help me please?
No one bothers to ask of me,
'Rachel' dear, 'What do you need?'

G Hailwood

Reflections

As I look out of my window and see the snow upon the ground.
There's a stillness creeping over me, not a soul or child around
No neighbour clearing up the path to make it safe to tread,
Or children offering to shop for fruit or veg. or bread.
My mind travels back over many years when I was just a lad,
My sisters three would help our ma and I would work with dad,
The fire blazing in the hearth, good food for us to eat,
Then when all our chores were done, we'd play in fields or street.
Our hoots and howls they could be heard but parents did just smile,
For it was safe for us to play, and we'd be back a while.

When knees were scraped, and hands were black, and day crept into
night
We'd sneak back home and try to wash before mum saw the sight
Then we'd all sit down together to eat stew and her plum duff
No TV tray upon our lap to eat that convenience stuff!
We'd talk about our time at school or maybe read a book,
And our parents they had time for us, the girls would learn to cook,
And boys would learn to change a wheel or maybe paint a chair
We hadn't lots of money, but then folk had time to care.
But now we hear such dreadful tales, of those who're getting old
With no-one knowing they are there. They're dying in the cold

There's youngsters living in boxes, sheltering from rain and snow
What chance have they of family life, and seeing their children grow,
There wouldn't be the suffering and people in such pain
If those old times came back to us and society cared again,
If each and every one of us would care for just one other,
A neighbour, brother, sister, friend, or someone else's mother
We should show by our example the love that's in our heart
And win the young folk back to us so they would play their part,
To make this world a better place, in which we all can share
Then see the end of suffering, for I'm sure we still must care.

F Watkinson

The Invader

It came in from the garden
To terrorise the house.
A beast like this I'd never seen
It was neither rat nor mouse.
It's eyes they were like saucers
As they searched around for bread,
The mouth it kept on opening
And filled my heart with dread.
And as it stood in front of me,
I examined it with care,
And underneath the cake of mud
I saw a crop of hair.
Its eyes they glinted at me
As it clutched a current bun,
I recognised the fearful beast
It was my hungry son.

James Cooke

Forbidden Love

If you could only realise, my very dearest dear,
How much, these last few months have filled my heart with joy,
                                        sincere,
If you could know, how much my heart, is filled with love for you,
My soul, and mind, enriched, by every little thing you do.
If you could see within my heart, and know that every beat
Is doubled in it's magnitude, the moment that we meet.
If you could read behind my eyes, my thoughts for you alone.
And know, that you have filled my heart, with joy, I've never
                                        known,
If you, could but, accept the love, that my heart feels for you.
Your heart might also, skip a beat, your soul start singing too.
If you and I could be as one, as fate, maybe, designs.
Intoxication we might feel, much more than felt from wines.
If you could only give, my love, as I would give to you.
And make the word belonging have a special meaning too.
If you and I could but forget, our lives are not our own.
Forget, to others we belong, and to them must atone.
But, you and I, my dearest dear, are of a special breed.
We cannot turn our back on trust, and hurt the ones who need.
And I, my love, am filled with joy, that you are such a man.
How could I love a spineless male, who takes love, where he can.
So, till the day fate may decree, that we are free to love,
Please keep me safe, within your heart, and say, all else above.
That you will never leave my life, That near me, you will stay,
Until the day, when we are gone, When no more debts, we'll pay,
Then I, my love, will live my life, with skies forever blue,
Knowing that, somehow, somewhere, my thoughts are shared, by
                                        you.

Alma Frame

Forget

Forget his name, forget his face.
Forget his smile, his warm embrace.
Forget the love that you once knew,
Remember now, she loves him too.

Forget the love that you once shared,
Forget the fact that he once cared.
Forget the times spent together,
Remember now, he's gone forever.

Forget him when they play your song,
Forget you cried the whole night long.
Forget how close you two once were,
Remember now, he's chosen her.

Forget his gentle little ways,
Forget you saw him yesterday.
Forget the things he used to do,
Remember now, she loves him too.

Forget the way he held your hand,
Forget the sweet things if you can.
Forget he said he'd leave you never,
Remember now, he's gone forever.

Forget the thrill when he walked by,
Forget the times he made you cry.
Forget the way he spoke your name,
Remember now, it's not the same.

Forget the hours on the phone,
Forget the times with him alone.
Forget the things he used to say,
Remember now, he's gone away.

Forget the time when you once knew,
That you loved him and he loved you.
Forget the thought it would last forever,
Remember now, that they're together.

Jane Craig

Angry

When I'm angry, I feel mad
Mad, not very glad
I shout and slam doors
and stomp my feet very hard on the floors
I fling things out of my way
to make them see I don't want to play!
I bang and scream
I be very mean
I even hide my face
so I can't be seen!
Anger!
Yes, *Anger!*
That's when I'm *Mad!*

Clare-Louise Cummins

Remembering....Remembering

Every night I think of him,
And every night I know
That I would give my soul
To travel back to long ago.

That all consuming passion
Which swept us on a tide,
Through golden days of living,
Of love we could not hide.

He filled my arms with roses,
Crashing music, heady wine -
Softly moving beams of moonlight,
The old clock marking time.

Helpless with shared laughter,
Overwhelming sudden tears.
The need for urgent talking,
Gentle comfort in my fears.

Year followed year, sweet harmony,
And passion still held sway.
But the cruel Elves of Circumstance
They always make you pay.

So high we stood upon the peak,
It was too far to fall,
And when the glorious bubble burst
He did not hear me call.

Now every night I think of him
I hear the wise men say,
I gave my soul long years ago
To make me rich today.
Sheila Griffin

Untitled

Quietly, softly on padded paws
With feet that hide protective claws
They glide across the open spaces
To show the World their feline faces.

Their coats are very smooth and sleek
And as we know they cannot speak
But always get our best attention
When they respond with their affection.

The fur is washed and often preened
Ensuring every inch is cleaned
To spend their time in sedate moods
Waiting for their favourite foods.

From us as friends they always choose
Knowing they will never lose
The love and fondest we show them how
And in response the cats meow.

No great demands but expectations
For the basic need of good relations
Between a cat and most of us
Without arousing too much fuss.

To be content, to sit and purr
Develops a bond that may be rare
And shows whilst on your lap or mat
A real true friend that is your Cat.

G A Johnson

Those Devils That he Never Saw

He couldn't sleep at nights, my dad,
For fear of submarines.
They'd glide through his sub-consciousness,
Torpedoing his dreams.
It frightened him for six long years
¡Their presence there below.
On every sea and ocean,
Over every wave he'd go.

Like devils that he never saw,
Like sheepdogs in control.
His every thought was monitored,
His mind was on parole.
Both sun and moon, would come and go,
And change horizon's look.
But all the beauty that was there,
Those silent devils took.

He's sixty-eight today: and had -
Another heart attack.
And I could see within his eyes,
The submarines were back.
An ever present torture took -
His life with every breath.
Those devils that he never saw
Were present at his death.

David Small

Fire My Soul

Embers glow, but slowly die,
Fading with the softest cry,
Gasp for air, to hold a flame,
Raging fire, now so tame,

Licking flames, burning deep,
Once a harvest you did reep,
Searing heat, caught my soul,
Drove me on, took control,

Warming with a hope to grow,
Blazing seeds of truth to know,
Guiding with the spark of life,
Catch the wind and set alight,

From the ashes, rise to meet,
Breath of life, be complete,
Kindle flames, new not old,
Light my life, fire my soul.

David Kerrick

Sleep Walk

I left her one morning
and walking away
I asked an old man
to show me the way

He said, 'that way's best
If you follow the wood',
and I left him right there
in the field where he stood

and day after day
and year after year
I stuck to that path
and never did veer

till one nice fine day
while feeling great hearted
I found myself
at the place where I'd started

and finding my love
still asleep in the bed
I quietly got in
and lay down my head

and just as I did
She woke up and said
'I see you've came back
I thought you were dead'

I looked at her guiltily
'What do you mean?'
'Don't worry' she said
'It was only a dream'
Martin Jackman

On Silloth Front

The crowds are gone from Silloth front.
The hazy hills of Scotland sleep again.
Winter's first chills begin to bite
And Solway's waters don their coat of grey.
A solitary walker leads his dog,
Unleashes it upon the grassy flats
And throws a ball afar for it to chase.
None to disturb, no sleeping sunbather
To voice complaint. The field is his.
Then stealing silently upon the scene
A fishing boat appears, and then another
And a third, making their stately way,
Stopping, turning, then resuming course
With following of eager herring gulls,
Wheeling and dipping, their raucous cries
Lost upon the wind and waves.
All is silent and the lofty pines
Brood upon the vanished throng,
Relieved to find again their wintry peace
But - truth to tell - a little sad as well.

Bryan Thompson

Time for a Laugh

'Get me a potato clock,'
Hubby said to me last night,
So as not to show my ignorance
I said to him 'all right'
Well, next day at a jewellers
I just popped in to ask
If they'd sell me a potato clock,
That set them all a task!
They had clocks with full cathedral chimes
And clocks with liquid quartz,
Clocks that even made the tea
And lots of other sorts.
They had small clocks, hall clocks, kitchen clocks
And clocks that go in ships,
But the nearest to a potato clock
Was one with micro chips.
In every jewellers that I went
They checked through all their stock
And after lengthy searching found
Not *One potato* clock!
That night I told my better half
Of the trouble that I'd had
He doubled up in laughter,
I thought he'd gone quite mad.
He then went on to tell me
What he wanted me to do,
Was to get him 'up at eight o'clock
Instead of quarter to!

Y Marsh

Why?

Why did he go,
Why did he leave.
Why did my man want to deceive.
I loved that man with all my heart
I never thought that we would part.

He's had the best years of my life
Why did he want me for his wife.
I cooked his meals and cleaned his house
And now he has another spouse.

I doubt she'll love him as much as I
I feel so sad that I could cry.
I lie awake for hours on end
How I'd love my marriage to mend.
If it wasn't for my daughters four
I'd want to die, of that I'm sure.

To me they are a tower of strength
For them I'd go to any length.
I love them like I loved their Dad
I wonder why he turned so bad.
If only he knew the harm he'd done
When he left me for another one.

He's shattered my faith, he's broke my heart
How I wish we weren't apart.
My marriage vows I'd make again
But next time, God, spare me the pain.

I never thought, when I said yes
My marriage would end in such a mess.
All I wanted from this life
Was to end my days as Gordon's wife.
For reasons that I'll never know
Gordon felt he had to go...

Joan Beer

A Fairy Tale in Rhyme

Sir - what a lovely gesture, and to many it is more like fairy tales
As we are being honoured by Her Royal Highness, the Princess of
Wales.
This little town has made renown,
By heritage old and new.
It is quite an honour to have the Royals passing through,
it is a day for celebrating, and merry making too.
The little town will be on the alert, and so will the boys in blue.
She will be more than welcome, if I know Wigan Town,
They are the kind of people who never let you down.

Just a small tribute to our Royal visitor.

E Reddington

A Woman's Lot

You know it's hard sharing my life
Being somebody's mother and somebody's wife
Sometimes I yearn, long to be free
Where is the girl who used to be me?
In the beginning I became we
Then all of a sudden two became three
It's always the same, the shout is for mum
There's never a day when my work is done
I look around and contemplate
The trials of life and the choices we make
And wonder what happened to liberation
Did it escape this generation?
'You play golf, dear and I'll do the dishes'
Oh what joy being Mr and Mrs
When I look around and reminisce
Is that what they meant by wedded bliss?
So in conclusion, like it or not
This will always be a woman's lot.

Angela Carlyle

Western Glory

Words cannot express the beautious wonder.
Miles of ever changing scenes
Russet mountains, woodlands splendour
Differing hues, browns, blues and greens.
The orange groves, desert flowering cacti.
Magical glorious land
'Blue Pacific'. 'The Grand Canyon',
Exquisite beauty, all in Gods hand.

Mary B Tyrer

Dreams

'What would you do' I asked my Dad
'If you won the pools and could have your dream?

He replied

'A house of my own where the air is clean
A bathroom, a fridge and washing machine
In a place where mills don't belch smoke all day.
And there's plenty of space for you to play.
'That's my dream'

What would I tell my children
If they asked the same of me?
For the things that were out of reach for dad
Are my reality

A yacht of my own, a villa in Spain.
A trip round the world by luxury plane,
A second, car double glazing

Honestly it's amazing
We are always wanting more, it seems,
Or maybe a man has need of dreams.

Marion Whelan

Memories

Like spinning tops the space machines fly round and round and
                                                        round.
Setting no special time or place for coming down to ground.
Yet, if we hear a voice, a tune, or see a loving face,
Our memory covers years and time at twice the flying pace.

Filed away in our memory box in a very special way,
Are all the treasures we discover as we travel life's long way.
School days, work days, romance love and marriage,
The magic drive on a moonlit night in an old fashioned horse and
                                                        carriage.

Remembering the very first glimpse of a brand new son or daughter,
Birthday parties filled with joy and happy children's laughter.
Memories too of fears and prayers when a loved one was in danger,
Promising all sorts of things to Him born in a manager

Memories of good holidays that passed so very quick,
Sailing to the Isle of Man and feeling oh! so sick.
Memories of a love so true that has stood the test of time,
Memories that are special just for you, and you and you.

The twilight years bring rest and peace, new memories for our store,
Our memory box is never full there's always room for more,
To sit and share all these good things with the younger generation
Is either fate or destiny that God granted every nation.

Death does not part two loving hearts from thought or word or deed,
Day by day the time draws near when the two once more shall meet.
So listen well to memories that are still so crystal clear,
Of all we do or do not in all our living years.

E Clucas

Robot Man

He was born of a woman upon plant earth
This man they call Robot who was human at birth.
He grew up to a man in the second world war
Raids and destruction had taken their score.

Industry next took him apart
Replacing his brain, his reason and heart
All of the pressure soon took it's toll
Making him into this mechanical doll.

He worked to a time switch to earn his pay
On the day or night shift he lived out each day.
No creativity at all. No beauty to be found
Just riding each day on works merry-go-round.

Slowly the work ground to a halt
Not knowing why: was it his fault?
Redundant! No. This cannot be.
They can't sack the likes of me.

He is now an old man although in his prime
Worn out with hard work and pressure and time.
He no longer thinks. His brain doesn't work
Each day is a nightmare he tries hard to shirk.

He rises at eight and eats what he can
Then stares at the box; this robot man
Every days is the same to this mechanised man
His only function, to do not to plan.

No dream has he. No present or past
Just motivate. Make the time last.
He never deviates from the routine, daily plan
Always the same. This robot man.
Freda Renton

Autumn in the Isle of Man

The golden gorse gives way to purple heather
As summer's sun in autumn's orange dress
Climbs later from her bed in misty mornings
And earlier returns, the night to bless.

The drowsy, humming bee, with duties calling,
Now turns from clover lawn to heather hill
And through cold-sharpened air on windy tussocks
Brings home sweet pollen, honey-pots to fill.

The grey and choppy sea with stormy humours
Denies the balmy blue of former days,
Reflecting heaven's thicker winter blanket
Which muffles up the warmth of sunshine rays.

The writhing mists creep slowly round the island
Like ghostly fingers, clammy, damp and cold;
As autumn's painter wipes out summer's colours,
Erasing ocean blue and sunshine gold.

Instead, he paints the isle with mellow beauty
In shades of bracken brown and misty grey
With purple, pink, and winter-green-clad hillsides
And orange-tinted sun to shine by day.

And old Mannanin throws his cloak around him
More often as the autumn days draw on,
Protecting fairy children, island dwellers,
Now all the hordes of visitors are gone.

Maureen Mitchell

Broken Circle

Baby girl in holy water
Wet cross dries
Happy Father

Teenage girl reaffirms vows
Happy proud people
pray behind pews

Young woman with gold cross
between her breasts
When she bathes in unholy water
Jesus sees her at her best

Laughing priest receives
confessions of young woman
express her needs

Young mother upholds vows
thinks of creation
child accepts pious views

Mother sees child refuse to confirm
understanding
refuses to condemn

Old woman lied on earth
now lies within
a worm crosses her smile

C X Moran

The City

Matchbox buildings piled up high,
Almost crowding out the sky;
From their lofty windows one can gaze
Onto an endless concrete maze,
Full of teeming millions who jostle and push,
And vie with the traffic's noise and rush;
Beetle-like cars shimmer and gleam,
Surging forward in a continuous stream.
The underground, a cavernous pit,
Swallows the people into it.
Humming it's own peculiar song,
An electric train glides along,
Bearing passengers to offices grey,
Where they're imprisoned for the day.
Others journey to the factory floor,
Only to suffer the machinery's roar.
In the city centre, 'midst the hectic scene,
Rests a tiny island of refreshing green;
Sporting flower beds and old stone seats,
There, many a fugitive retreats.
As dusk arrives, neon signs flash and wink,
Hypnotising the public, between each blink,
Into visiting theatres, cinemas, and clubs,
Cafes, restaurants and pubs.
Gradually, the city's heart slows its pace,
Gaining strength for tomorrow's race.
When the golden dawn starts to peep.
Weary nightworkers, go home to sleep;
For the remainder, a new day begins,
Once more the progressive city 'wins'.

Bernice Grocott

Troubled

Often when I sit alone,
I think of the world outside.
A cruel place I'm so afraid,
I want to go and hide.

a coward I am not I feel,
For up to things I face,
Yet my heart bleeds, what can I do?
How can I help eraze?

The cruel things man does to man,
And in the name of what?
God? Progress? Love? or Hate?
Is this to be our Lot?

Though in this sea of humanity,
I am as a single grain.
If, though my days, I try to not,
Bring to my fellows pain

I can, by example, show my son,
The way things should be done.
And hope and pray that some day soon,
Jehovahs will be done.

Christina Myers

Untitled

You know that one day God prepares, a room in Heaven above,
A place for your dear Mother, and he'll care for her with love.
You know that it will happen, and yet when that time arrives,
You feel your heart is breaking, and the tears will sting your eyes.

But she hasn't gone forever, and she isn't far away,
She'll be watching over all of you, and be with you every day.
She'll help you through your sorrow, and hold you when you weep,
You'll see her in your dreams, as she's with you when you sleep.

So please don't feel resentment, it's the way that God has planned,
And when it's our time also, he will take us by the hand,
To the place he has prepared for us, where the sun will always shine,
And the Mother that you thought you'd lost, is there waiting all the
time.

Rita Pendlebury

Chaos

Living in a room with the world outside,
in solitude prefer to hide,
from all the chaos on the street,
a fire burns, I feel the heat.
Recession takes its toll,
the end of all control,
anarchy is all around,
all my friends are going down.
Hot head ghetto, know no fear,
down so long they just don't care,
absorbed so much, a heavy load,
stand back, watch it all explode.
Running battles, war and trouble,
corpses found amongst the rubble.
Governments forever doing,
look out, watch out, a fires brewing.
Dread has filled their hearts with doubt,
how long before it all comes out?
A blaze with no control,
the law has lost it's hold.
As we walk into the future hold my hand,
As chaos comes to rule upon this land.

D Pritchard

Romance

We met in Spring, Romance's wing
Moved as you came and fanned love's flame.
All Summer through you came to woo,
And life was sweet, our love complete.
My heart was true, but what of you?
I thought you cared, that love was shared.
Your ardent lips, your fingertips
Caressing mine, heady as wine.
Came Autumn on and you were gone,
And I was left, my heart bereft.
All Winter through I cried for you,
In vain did yearn for your return.
Springtime again brought love's refrain,
And hopes anew for love more true,
That will not fade with Autumn's shade,
But stronger grow through Winter's snow.

K M Dobson

When Grandma Came to Stay

I liked Grandma coming to stay with us,
She was cheerful and easy to please,
She was interested in everything,
And she always put us at our ease.

'Joe has changed his job,
Mary's had a baby
Sue's got a boyfriend now,
And Michael's joined the navy,

I liked to hear about the old days,
And the people she had known,
How they did things then,
And 'oh how time had flown.'

We would go out on Sunday afternoon,
To the country or by the sea,
Sometimes we would go blackberry picking,
Which Gran enjoyed as much as me.

'Look how many I have picked'.
I would have to boast,
But when we got home,
We'd find Gran had picked the most.

Each evening we would play cards,
Gran would take the lead,
Then from the bible,
A chapter she would read.

'Well God had his blessing',
She would always say,
She was a dear old lady,
I wish she was here to-day.
Violet Astbury

Do You Know Who You Are

(This poem was inspired by Paul McCartneys 'Ghosts of the Past',
shown at Liverpool Anglican Cathedral last year.)

Give up pretending, delay the ending
Bring a bright day - forget the confusion
Dream the illusion, all the sweet way

Think of the future, bring dreams to mind
Will there be interest - leave hate behind.

Living free, come to me, living peace
Love increase
Where did our senses go, where did the
feeling flow

Do you know who you are,
As you lie there sleeping
Do you see in your dreams
A child who is weeping.

And the dark side of life
Is far to much to bear
For one so very young
- But I will be there

I'll never leave you, give me this moment
Of time - not discord coming
Through the air.

Sending a message, through a night wild
Casting a shadow, but must save the child

Live in me, live in me
I will live on through you
After years of nothingness
A mighty love comes through

Hear me, hear me - why do you never hear me
Are you surprised to find
The sky's still there
And we're not blind.

M Hulme

Beginnings

I have caught a butterfly in my hands
Frail-winged, velvet textured,
A graceful splash of coloured light.
If attentive, I can feel
Cobweb'd wings, quietly quivering.

Fear not, for my hands are delicate
And my unfolded fingers will let you fly,
Those tremulous wings - lightening upon blue air
A chaotic, colour - filled flight of joy; -
And you do know,
That if you should tire,
You can return, and rest once more,
Closing your wings in my enclosed hands.

Nicholas Russell

Just Passing By

I see the passing faces
Of people walking by
But many seem unhappy
I often wonder why.

I wonder what they're thinking
And why they look so sad
When life can be so happy,
It's really not that bad.

I sit here in my wheelchair
To watch the passers by
Just wishing I could also walk,
Sometimes I even try.

But I am very lucky
For *happiness* I know
Refusing always in my life
To let the sadness show.

Pauline Laura Bates

Chester Beside the Dee

The sun cast shadows long,
The breeze was soft, a sleepy song,
And people strolled beside the Dee,
Ice creams cool or afternoon tea.

The gardens dripped in splendour,
A collage of colours rich and tender,
The whites and the blues,
Amongst indigo hues.

The yellows and reds,
Blasting through their earthen beds,
And the grass lay the accolade,
To all the beauty that was on parade.

And the river drifted like the day,
Leaving reflections as it slipped away,
As thoughts were carried in the breeze,
And made the gentle rustle of the trees.

Stephen Ebbrell

Anniversary Dinner

For three whole years we've been together
And shared each precious minute
My life just wouldn't be the same
If you were not there, in it
We've had our up's, we've had our downs
We've had our share of worry,
So to celebrate our special day
I've made us both a curry!

Myra Johnston

Untitled

Emerald were the leaves
That once I knew.
Graceful were the trees
That here once grew.

Richly coloured blades
Swayed in the breeze.
Greens, reds of all shades,
Now gone are the trees.

Buttercup yellows and brown,
Copper, bronze and gold.
As glistening jewels in a crown.
The trees, their stories told.

Stories of wisdom and might,
The great oak and birch did tell.
Of sunny days, in the darkness of night,
Until the historic statues fell.

In my mind I hold them.
Clearly I see them still
In their coloured Autumn cloaks,
For my heart and soul to fill.

A M Hogg

Amy Goodfornothing 1892 - 1986

Amy Goodfornothing,
   so her son remarked
      to the undertaker,

Had been really,
   as her name suggests,
      good at nothing:

Couldn't add up,
   couldn't spell,
      'Reading? A waste of time.'

Son Goodfornothing
   gave some of Amy's
      handiwork in lace -

A table-cloth,
   twelve serviettes
      and some handkerchiefs -

To an antique stall
   where they sold for
      nine hundred and fifty pounds
         seventy-five pence.

Norah Mortimer

The Sun Worshipper

I stretch, languorous in the sun
The balmy breeze riffles my hair
Butterflies dip and swoop in fun
Through the clover scented air.

Luxuriantly I tauten my limbs
And watch my toes involuntary twitch
Like separate entities, acting on whims,
And I lie silent as a witch.

And from the corner of my eye
As I manicure and tend my nails
I see the birds in the harebell sky
And looking down I see the snails.

These curious creatures go so slow
Toting caravans upon their backs
As if they have nowhere to go
What inconsequential facts.

Divers thoughts my mind beguile
Too warm and lazy to worry
I'll lie here a little while
There really is no hurry.

I lick my shoulder to feel it's taste
The sun's glow drowses me
A dragon-fly whirrs past in haste
My green eyes flicker as they see.

Loud voices shatter the tranquil air
'Oh look darling, what is that?'
I rouse, prick up my ears, and purr
'Don't fret, it's only a cat.'
Stella Worden

Dream On

All my life I've dreamed of being something that I'm not,
A snooker star, a footballer, a raconteur, a swot,
I've dreamed of playing cricket, batting with David Gower,
I'd practice in the garden, for hour after hour,

I wanted to be a business man, making millions out of stocks,
Or a famous fashion designer, making ladies frilly frocks,
A jockey in the Derby, pipping Lester at the post,
Giving high society parties, where I could be mine host,

An actor in the theatre, in stunning costume dramas,
Drive tractors in rush-hour, just like other farmers,
Working for the BBC, as a high brow quiz presenter,
But I'd gladly sacrifice the lot, to be a great inventor,

Of course all my inventions would benefit mankind,
Labour saving devices so life's not such a bind,
I've invented a shelving system, self-assembly even by fools,
The whole task could be completed, without the use of tools,

Money would simply pour in, we'd make more than we could spend,
I could realise an ambition, and buy myself a friend,
My wife said, let's get busy, drawing plans and all that stuff,
So I pointed out quite rightly, I'm an inventor, thats enough,

It's really up to others to bring things to fruition,
I'm just the ideas man, thinking, that's my mission,
She'd have me working night and day, hour after hour,
I've got to get my beauty sleep, and dream of David Gower!

Les Eckersley

Memory

She's like a lovely summer's day,
The sunshine that has flown;
She like a rose in early June,
This memory, that I own.

She's like the early morning dew,
Refreshing as the rain;
She's like the daffodil's in spring,
And, memory is her name!

She's like a blueness of the sea,
She's like a bird, so bright and free;
She's like the star, that flies thro' space,
She's memory, she is grace.

She's laughter, sadness, joy and tears,
She's there beside us, thro' the years;
She reflects the past, like a crystal mere,
She's memory, vast and clear.

She's like the view, from on y'on hill,
She's like the plain, the lake, so still,
She's like the green of, y'on huge tree,
She's evergreen, she's memory.

Bert Latham

God's Country

My memory a story, financial survivors
No place then for money men or financial advisers
And disinterest in interest and the upwardly mobile
With laughter our master, contentment our profile

How eager the meagre, they offered their good
In this land I called homeland in the time of childhood
They taught me of family but to help each and sundry
Understand my own land, I knew as God's country

A contrast with what's past, our remote controlled roles
Fax machines, TV screens, with remote controlled souls
When the ad men are glad men, to look not at themselves
Persuade us true happiness, lies on Sainsbury's shelves

This shire of desire, mans a yearn to return
To the simple, God's people, a man's yearn to re-learn
As before, heavens door is a love of mankind
For surely, God's country, is a state of man's mind

In God's place, our rat race, will remain in reserve
In each other, we suffer the disdain we deserve
My penance, my absence, from this place I know well
My reward, am restored, resurrection from hell.

Graham Hilditch

The Dealer (Hustler)

The bravest man of all is he who walks towards his goal
For none of us are given to know which way the dice will fall.
And as we cast our lot upon the gaming board of life
We can't know which way the cards will turn, towards happiness or
                                                            strife,
Aces high, the Jacks our fool, the Queen of Hearts our friend
What cards will on the table lie when the game is at an end,
The rules laid down so long ago make losers of us all
The Devil deals the fastest hand, his stake's the dreamers soul.
He rolls the dice or turns a card at every step you take
Waits around the corner to open Hells dark gate,
You need to play the game right, watch each move he makes
You can see when Old Nick's cheating, it's written on his face,
He'll squint his eyes and glance around; shuffle both his hoofs
Watch the horses racing as he plans another move,
Swish his tail from side to side, slowly grind his teeth
You hope for just one simple slip to gain some blessed relief,
Search your mind for prayers or rhymes to still his endless game
Down another whiskey, open another vein, spill the blood of ages
past wrapped in a pagan prayer
Look for Gods and heroes who were never really there,
For all there is is you and he in a never ending maze
Following each other round in a drifting smoke-filled haze,
For he is you and you are he and both they are each other
Joined in the dance of life and death, man and his demon brother,
So wait awhile and hold those cards the ones you dealt before,
You hold three aces and a king the Devil's next to draw
He takes a card, the Jack of spades, fate lies in your hands
Who will play the Devil next if you now fail to score,
One more card another King once more a twisted hand
Another time, another game, play on, may fate be damned.

Toni Wright

123

Half a Pound of Happiness

Good morning, Sir - can I help you?

Yes, Miss -
I would like a small piece of happiness please - about half a pound.

Half a pound, Sir?

Yes, please.

Sorry! ---

This is the right counter, isn't it?

Yes. -

Well, I must say, it is getting worse!
I came last week and you told me it was on order.

Yes, I know -
they've sent everything else - sadness, pain, illusion, fear....
you know - the usual.
French is your favourite, isn't it? - or was it Dutch?

I don't mind - any really.

Never mind, love!
Try again next week -
I'll keep a piece under the counter for you -
should it arrive unexpectedly.
Could do with some myself, to tell you the truth.

Alfa

The Robed Hunter of Love Rides Within the Wood

The golden shining rays of Spring
Stream now in all my dearest deepest dreams
Among the great trees of every forest's green

For she has lent her shimmering gems
To jewel the hauberk of the happy hunter
Who rides his horse now among the boughs
And branches of all the broadest oaks

She has spun celestial robes for her love
To wind around her own sweet singer
For he will never flee her
His melodies seep forever
With every single holy hue and careful colour
She has laid with tender heart upon his limbs

Through all the spiritual seasons
He will stay there
Sealed by leafy bars of love's own prison
While silly crowds will laugh
At what they see
As all his lonely slavery
In vain their horrid hearts would strip
The garment of God and gown of glory
Love granted him

But I shall smile and greet all happily
Mad with mirth that they will never know
I would sooner see the grave
Among this god-like green
Then lose the soft warm rapture
Of the raiment she was woven
Upon her love-wound loom
And that her deft and fair fingers
In one blessed night gave me.

Jason Redvers Latham

Turkish Delight

Cool wind blew through her golden hair
Breeze settled still on her lips
He held his hand upon her face
And gasped a breath of Gypsies kiss.

Two bodies swaying from side to side
Lost in each others passion
Their emotions explode with tender love
Time stood still as they experienced heaven.

Fire in their eyes and burning hearts
Whispering their deepest desires
The whole world sleeps through the cries of delight
They know no boundaries of pleasure.

Mary-Louise Currell

I Stood Alone

I stood alone amidst concrete, brick, and broken glass,
Mud and weed, and unmowed grass,
Wet leaves and litter on the floor,
Boarded window, bricked up door.

I stood alone in hazy pollution of silent midday
Momentary sun shinning on a depressed estates decay,
Despair manifest, integrity to God put to the test,
A mind a vortex of unrest.

I stood alone and knocked on a door,
Looking for solace, feeling footsore,
Looking for security amidst mental turmoil,
Among unseen demons looking for spoil.

Robert Halton

Injured By Love

I play my song of love that hurts and read the same thing in my book
But when you love with all your heart you have to leap before you
look.
I know it pays to think things through but love demands a blinded
faith
Like leaping forward in the dark or walking into empty space.
As time goes on sensation grows, the hurt has sharper claws to use.
The hurt that comes from lack of thought; the pain caused by such
hard abuse.
The answer 'No' can often sting but does not have the lasting pain
Of meetings missed and calls not made or words unkept time and
again.
I ask myself if it is worth the misery you put me through.
I'd like to say that it is not but know I won't because it's you.
The only way to cure this ache is leave it all - both good and bad.
I sometimes feel that's what I want but then I think I must be mad.
I'll stick around and wait my turn for those rare times when your love
shows.
I'll take the pain, bite back the tears though why I do God only
knows.

Keith McDonnell

An English Country Lane

Not for me the glitter of Paris nights,
Or the heat of the high Spanish sun,
Not for me the grandeur of canyons
And gorge's where great rivers run.

But give me a lane in this England
And a ditch where meadow sweet grows,
Where harebells and hawkbit side by side
Chalk colours an artist knows.

Give me willows that shade the stream
Where moorhens seek their nightly rest
And starry stitchwort peeps behind
The grass where willow warblers nest.

A morning where speedwell lifts its face
To welcome the life-giving sun
Is worth to me a thousand nights
Where cacti thirst and gophers run.

Gladys Bevan

Grandad One-Tooth Baby-sitting
-in memory of Abraham Phillips-

Near-deaf, he had the volume up to full
and leaned his nodding head towards the screen:
Wayne or Cagney, Bogart, Steve McQueen...
he loved the swagger of the Saturday night
hard men. I sat with him
beyond bedtime, led
into a world of guns and girls
and happy endings. The picture was always black-and-white.

If I gave trouble his Linfield lilt would tell
of horrors behind the curtains. The pallid faces
of eyeless bogeymen from rotting, evil places.
Scuttling, bodiless hands. The ghost
of Buck Ruxton, gory with the traces
of murder. The words
he used stirred
me to fearful fascination and I fell
into line. The world outside was monsters and devils and worse.

Jinny Green-Teeth lurked beneath the Lune,
he said, his one tooth chewing on the smoke
from a Park Drive. His pub-stained shock
of white hair was like the floss
of a dirty cloud in summer. As he spoke
his dead eye
was dull as a dry
pebble. His other shone
with wicked life. He said she ate naughty boys.

Only last night the long muddy
Lune belched Jinny into my dreams,
and every button summons bogeypeople onto the TV screen.

Ivan Phillips

Visions of Life

As soothing darkness falls,
It leads me to the quiet halls,
Where I used to play,
On a cooling summer's day,
When I was young,
My life still not sung,
A child in every way.

Since then long years have past,
The world is changing fast.
Now I have shaped tomorrow,
With all its joy and sorrow.
An older face,
A different place,
My own road I must follow.

Still I ache to touch the sun,
With dreams of things yet not done,
Of journeys which I have not made,
Of paradise which does not fade.
My whispered words,
Like gentle birds,
Seek not to be afraid.

As every new day dawns,
I struggle with its rose like thorns,
So the flower I may see,
And through my dreams be set free.
A hope, a prayer,
A heart felt care,
This is my destiny.

M Malone

Beach Concentrics

Dreaming merry-go-rounds on sunshine days,
About laughing, crescendo-type girls, and the ways
That an eagle will follow a path to the sun
While the envious trees look like spiders have spun
A criss-cross of branches, to catch those who'd dare
To climb to the top, just to catch the stars there.
Then a lost little boy, with an ice cream face,
Is screaming for Mother, in hop's he'll disgrace
The parents of a child with a dubious past.
Till the noise fades away, and the dreamer at last
Is left with the seagulls, the silence to hear.
Like the whisper of waves when no footsteps are near.
The lure of the fun-fair, the smell of the crowds.
The candy-floss models of big candy clouds,
The sensation of sun, and it's nice, burning pain.
The dreamer awakes now, it's started to rain.

A Leather

133

Complements

My twin and I
Are opposites,
As certain as can be,
Just as waves are,
To the calm,
Yet both make up the sea.

My twin and I
Are opposites,
As sure as sure can be,
We are ourselves,
But, now and then,
I'm her, and she is me!

Jennifer Marsh

England

Sandy lanes meander through patchwork fields,
Hedgerows of blues, yellows, whites and reds,
Foxes and badgers searching out their needs,
Cabbage whites flitter amongst grower's beds.
Rivers and streams babbling thro' leafy glen,
Whilst wood pigeons coo in searching flight,
The nightingale's melodious song warbles when,
Lingering scents of sweet flowers fill heady night.
Lush pastures, green, 'neath cotton-wool skies,
Cuckoo's call sounds from coppice, or wood,
Hovering kestrel swoops, and field mouse cries!
Kingfisher dives as nothing else could.
Lazy mid-summer days keeping all at rest,
Clumsy, ambling reaper harvesting wheaten towers,
All help to remind us this land is still the best!
England! oh lovely England! this home of ours!

Jeff Stott

A - Z

Anxiously awaiting aside a
Beautiful broad
Cat-walk. Coloured
Dresses, delightful and delicious
Erotically and eligantly express
Fashion
Gracefulness, gorgeous girls, glamour and glitz
How much?
Impact
Jealousy but
Keep
Looking luxurious like
Marilyn Monroe, models
Noticed with
Outstanding
Perfection
Quickly
Rome round the
Stage, sly smiles, smart suits, standing
Tall in
Unnatural uniforms the
Value of vogue
Woman wanting what we are wearing all
Yearning with
Zeal.

Amy L Todd

Trees in Blossom

Lilac, laburnum and flowering cherry,
Magnificent trees in fine blossom bedecked.
Coloured perfection combining in splendour,
Enhancing our gardens with dazzling effect.

Gracefully dancing in soft, gentle zephyr,
Adorning each tree with a varying hue.
Vivid in contrast, or delicate shading,
When nature in springtime clothes each branch anew.

Renèe P Blackburn

137

Paradise Lost

The little wood was wider once,
It stretched a mile or more
Where oak and beech marched arm in arm
As far as Kentsford shore.
Their yearly gifts of leaves and fruit
Would make rich harvest store
For busy beetles, scurrying mice,
The squirrel and wild boar.

This remnant of its former pride
Defiant, holds at bay
The ranks of creeping bungalows
Fast gaining ground each day;
Whose formal gardens eat the land
Where rabbits used to play,
While, smirking in their pampered beds,
Fine roses make display.

I walked the woods again this Spring
To find the little dell
Where snowdrops and anemones
Abound. I knew it well.
But mounds of builders' rubbish choked
The site. Some infidel,
Proud in his private Paradise,
Makes earth and heaven rebel.

John Rowley

The Block

The block is every poets thief,
stealing our inspiration,
it is the chains that bind us,
to this earth that is our prison,
the block is the insecurity,
that lies in our hearts,
the pain of the past,
that clouds our future,
it is the darkness,
in which all our fears lie,
the impotence of mind,
that is the block.

Damian Wilford

The Pain of Losing You

If I lost you a rusty nail would pierce my heart
Stabbing, gouging, and the hole it made would never
Match the loss of you

I climbed a mountain, reached the volcano, jumped in
Into the abyss, for what.
You still was not there for me

If I lost you life would be a cripple, a hunchback.
A leper so alone
Alone in a world of momentary sorryness

I reached for another can, poured another dram of forgetfulness
Slipped into the darkness of stupor and slept, for what.
When I awoke you were not there for me

If I lost you time would have to accelerate
The future years on, would have to be now
To make you the past

I looked into the future there was me
Looking back into the past looking everywhere for you
But still you would not be there for me

If I lost you a nail would pierce my heart,
And rust there forever

B Roberts